I0418348

CHORDS OF
REDEMPTION

A Worship Leader's Story

LARRY BRISCOE

CHORDS OF REDEMPTION: A Worship Leader's Story

Copyright © 2025 Larry Briscoe

All rights reserved.

Scripture quotations in this publication are taken from the King James Version. Public domain.

ISBN: 979-8-9923197-4-3

TABLE OF CONTENTS

INTRODUCTION

In this compelling story, we follow the life of a man whose journey is marked by profound struggles, redemption, and the transformative power of faith. From his early days as a worship leader in a thriving mega-church to the harrowing experiences of addiction and incarceration. His story is one of resilience against overwhelming odds.

As he navigates the complexities of life, including family dynamics, personal aspirations, and the challenges of addiction, his faith remains a guiding light. His relationships with family and friends are tested, yet they also serve as a source of strength and support. The story dives into the impact of his choices, the consequences of his actions, and the eventual path to recovery and spiritual awakening.

Tragedy strikes, leading to a deep exploration of grief and healing. Through it all, the themes of love, forgiveness, and the quest for purpose resonate powerfully.

His legacy is ultimately one of hope, as he inspires others to seek redemption and embrace their faith, leaving an indelible mark on those around him. This story is a reminder of life's fragility and the human spirit's enduring strength.

CHAPTER 1: THE SNAKE

The morning air was thick with the stench of sweat and humidity, combined with the rattling and rumbling of a van navigating a bumpy highway. The man glanced down at his orange jumpsuit, jail flip-flops, and the shackles binding his hands to his feet. In his hands was a plastic bag containing two sandwiches: one filled with peanut butter (no jelly) and the other with an unidentifiable meat of the day.

The sound of fellow inmates munching on their sandwiches filled the van when one of them, speaking with a heavy Southern accent and a barely intelligible dialect, directed his gaze at the man. "Hey you," he said, his eyes narrowing. "I'm a trade my peanut butter for your meat sammich."

"No," the man replied defiantly, meeting the inmate's glare. This inmate, a lanky man in his forties, bore a striking resemblance to Charles Manson, his head and body covered with tattoos. "Then I'm a take it from you after I kill ya," the inmate threatened. The man thought to himself, "Yeah, right. He's as shackled as I am." The inmate continued, "I got nothin' to lose; I'm a be in here forever."

At that moment, the inmate began squirming in his seat like a snake, wriggling free from his shackles while the man watched in disbelief. There was nothing he could do as the situation escalated.

Suddenly, the inmate lunged across the van, wrapping his shackles around the man's throat. The man fought back, but his shackled hands and feet made his efforts futile.

1

Just as he felt himself slipping into unconsciousness from asphyxiation, the van began to slow down. The inmate abruptly halted his attack and retreated to his seat, skillfully reapplying his shackles. He then flashed the man a toothless grin, his beady red and yellow eyes glinting with malice. "We finish this lata," he taunted.

Proverbs 24:1-2 Speaks of evil people and their hearts of violence.

[1] *Be not thou envious against evil men, neither desire to be with them.*
[2] *For their heart studieth destruction, and their lips talk of mischief.*

The man now had the inmate's image permanently etched in his memory, including every tattoo and marking. The eye tattoos reading "Kill" on one side and "Him" on the other, along with various skulls and other ominous symbols, painted a portrait of a genuinely unlikable individual.

Trembling from fear and a lack of oxygen, the man's thoughts spiraled into despair as he realized this might be the grim reality of the rest of his life. Just four days ago, he had been the prominent worship leader in a thriving mega-church.

CHAPTER 2: GOD SPEAKS

Twenty-one years earlier, a four-year-old boy named Kenneth Bradford was introduced as the second of three sons in his family. His older brother was Daniel, followed by Ken, and then their younger brother, Chase. Ken is a typical child who adores Barney and has a gentle heart.

One evening, as Mom and Dad kissed the boys goodnight and tucked them into bed, young Ken announced, "God talked to me last night." Both parents responded as expected, "That's wonderful, Ken. Just keep saying your prayers."

During the same bedtime routine, Ken declared three weeks later, "God talked to me again last night." Curious, Dad asked Ken for more details about his conversation. "What do you think about Ken talking to God?" Dad inquired of Mom. They both agreed it was likely just a product of a four-year-old's imagination.

As Ken grew a little older, he spoke with his grandmother about God and assorted topics. I overheard her say, "Maybe you'll grow up to be a preacher someday." It's astonishing how his spirituality and love for God were already apparent even at such a tender age.

For several months, God continued to speak audibly to Ken. Imagine the extraordinary experience of having God audibly speak with you directly.

1 Kings 19:11-12 God speaks with a "still small voice" or "a delicate whispering voice."

[11] And he said, Go forth, and stand upon the mount before the Lord. And, behold, the Lord passed by, and a great and strong wind rent the mountains, and brake in pieces the rocks before the Lord; but the Lord was not in the wind: and after the wind an earthquake; but the Lord was not in the earthquake:
[12] And after the earthquake a fire; but the Lord was not in the fire: and after the fire a still small voice.

At age five, Ken experienced a rash accompanied by a high fever exceeding 104°. Despite the pediatrician's recommendation to place him in a lukewarm bath, his condition showed no improvement.

After several visits to the pediatrician, he was referred to a specialist renowned for his work in Juvenile Rheumatoid Arthritis (JRA), who diagnosed Ken with an early stage of the disease.

Despite the challenges posed by JRA, Ken used crutches intermittently for a couple of years but maintained a positive attitude throughout his struggles.

Jeremiah 29:11 God knows his plans for you.

[11] For I know the thoughts that I think toward you, saith the Lord, thoughts of peace, and not of evil, to give you an expected end.

The disease did not hinder Ken's passion for life. When his condition was managed, he actively participated in baseball, a love that lasted for many years and included All-Star tournaments.

A breakthrough medication, Embrel, was identified as an effective treatment for JRA. During his teenage years, Ken began receiving bi-weekly injections of Embrel, which significantly helped control his condition, although they came with serious side effects, including a reduction in his immune system's effectiveness.

Some may wonder, "Who sinned to have caused such a loving child to endure so much suffering?"

John 9:1-3 Jesus explains who sinned to cause a man to be born blind.

[1] And as Jesus passed by, he saw a man which was blind from his birth.

4

²And his disciples asked him, saying, Master, who did sin, this man, or his parents, that he was born blind?
³Jesus answered, Neither hath this man sinned, nor his parents: but that the works of God should be made manifest in him.

Image 1 Ken with his JRA doctor.

CHAPTER 3: THE DRUMMER BOY

Ken became interested in music as a young teenager when he received a drum set as a Christmas gift. Initially, he played the drums without any sense of rhythm or beat.

His older brother, Daniel, a talented guitar player, often had friends over to jam. One afternoon, a friend sat down at the drum set and taught Ken some basic beats, igniting his passion to enhance his drumming skills.

Ken had formed a garage band with his three best friends by eighth grade. Their musical abilities flourished, thanks in part to the encouragement and guidance of their music teacher, whose support and friendship extended beyond their high school years.

During an end-of-year celebration in their eighth-grade music class, the band performed a set of cover songs and officially named themselves "Fermata", a term in music notation that signifies a note should be held longer than its usual duration.

The band practiced diligently in the garage, writing and performing original music alongside their covers. However, their enthusiasm was met with anger from the neighbors, leading to multiple noise complaints and visits from the police.

To mitigate the noise issues, the band eventually moved their practice sessions to a back bedroom, which helped keep the volume in check. Parents of aspiring musicians can certainly relate to the challenges of managing noise levels.

One day, Ken told his dad, "I really want to play worship music." However, his aspiration to perform for the Lord did not materialize at once.

Genesis 4:21 Introduces Jubal a descendant of Cain, as the Father of Music.

²¹ And his brother's name was Jubal: he was the father of all such as handle the harp and organ.

The band began performing at local venues, gradually attracting a loyal following of friends. This trend continued throughout their high school years, leading to significant popularity. They ultimately gained recognition through various church youth ministries.

Although the band's original music was not explicitly worship-oriented, it resonated with young audiences and inspired them. They chose not to incorporate worship songs into their setlist, yet their appeal within youth ministries continued to grow.

At one point, the band secured a brief engagement with the Extreme Tour, a Christian-based initiative aimed at young teens. This tour was characterized by a profound commitment to their faith, with participants gathering for prayer and fellowship multiple times daily.

Psalm 95:1-3 A call to worship.

¹ O come, let us sing unto the Lord: let us make a joyful noise to the rock of our salvation.
² Let us come before his presence with thanksgiving, and make a joyful noise unto him with psalms.
³ For the Lord is a great God, and a great King above all gods.

The band performed together until they reached young adulthood. Eventually, they parted ways, as most members lost their passion for a life in music. However, Ken's love for music remained unwavering.

Image 2 First drum set.

Image 3 Fermata performing at a local venue.

CHAPTER 4: WORSHIP BEGINS

K en responded to an advertisement seeking a drummer. Much to his surprise the position was for a worship band within a couple's group at a local church. This opportunity fulfilled his aspiration to be part of a worship band.

The worship band and church exposed Ken to numerous ministers and the Christian influence he sought. Before long, he led worship while Daniel played guitar for a young adult ministry at the church.

Matthew 18:20 Gathering in His name, God is there.

20 For where two or three are gathered together in my name, there am I in the midst of them.

Ken later enrolled in a Christian college affiliated with the church, which further fueled his desire to deepen his understanding of God. The teachers, counselors, and professors had a wealth of biblical knowledge, and Ken eagerly absorbed their teachings.

When Ken or his father had inquiries about various aspects of the Bible, Ken would particularly seek the guidance of one professor. This professor held a PhD in Biblical Studies, and his expertise was remarkable.

2 Peter 1:2-7 Explains the growth in faith through knowledge of God

<u>*and Jesus,*</u>

²*Grace and peace be multiplied unto you through the knowledge of God, and of Jesus our Lord,*
³*According as his divine power hath given unto us all things that pertain unto life and godliness, through the knowledge of him that hath called us to glory and virtue:*
⁴*Whereby are given unto us exceeding great and precious promises: that by these ye might be partakers of the divine nature, having escaped the corruption that is in the world through lust.*
⁵*And beside this, giving all diligence, add to your faith virtue; and to virtue knowledge;*
⁶*And to knowledge temperance; and to temperance patience; and to patience godliness;*
⁷*And to godliness brotherly kindness; and to brotherly kindness charity.*

Ken excelled in leading worship for the young adult ministry. The worship band occasionally filled in for the Saturday evening service, and he also played drums for the main Sunday service at times.

His time at college was progressing well, and he was establishing a reputation within the church. It's important to note that this is a well-established mega-church.

Image 4 Worship band for the young adult ministry.

CHAPTER 5: THE CLEANER

One morning, Daniel burst into the house, claiming he had accidentally swallowed poison. Initially, Dad thought he was exaggerating but asked for an explanation. Daniel mentioned seeing a cup in Chase's truck that he thought was coffee, so he drank it.

Since Chase was the last to use the truck, Dad contacted him to find out what was in the cup. Chase revealed it contained commercial calcium and rust cleaner from his workplace.

Without delay, Dad and Daniel rushed to the emergency room, where Daniel was admitted. Though he tried to vomit, his stomach was empty.

The ER doctors attempted to pump his stomach, but it was unsuccessful, and his vital signs continued to deteriorate. Consequently, he was transferred by ambulance to a different hospital that was better equipped to manage his condition.

Following an upper endoscopy, the gastroenterologist spoke with the family. She explained that given the type of poison and the extent of the damage, there is over a 98% chance of not surviving.

The specialist showed the family endoscopy images, illustrating the extensive damage. The images clearly showed the charred interior, from his throat down to his stomach.

2 Corinthians 1:3-5 He comforts us in all our troubles.

³ Blessed be God, even the Father of our Lord Jesus Christ, the Father of mercies, and the God of all comfort;

⁴ Who comforteth us in all our tribulation, that we may be able to comfort them which are in any trouble, by the comfort wherewith we ourselves are comforted of God.

⁵ For as the sufferings of Christ abound in us, so our consolation also aboundeth by Christ.

The news shocked the family, making it difficult to comprehend. Daniel's mother requested a Catholic priest to pray for him.

Ken contacted the church, informing them of Daniel's critical condition. Soon, about 30 people gathered in the lobby, forming a prayer chain.

By the next morning, Ken and Daniel's dad joined the prayer chain, struggling to hold back tears during this emotional time.

Later that day, the doctors brought Daniel out of the induced coma so the family could visit. When he awoke, Daniel was confused and thought he was in China. He told his dad, "You came to China to see me." Despite the difficulty, his dad managed to chuckle at this.

To make matters worse, Daniel's eyes were entirely red. They looked quite severe, prompting the doctors to identify the issue. The condition, known as subconjunctival hemorrhage, occurs when blood vessels in the eyes break due to intense vomiting.

The doctors performed another endoscopy on Daniel and awaited the results. When the gastroenterologist returned, she had tears in her eyes. The charring was gone, replaced by healing pink tissue throughout his internal organs.

"This shows the power of prayer," the gastroenterologist said, fighting back tears with the family. She spoke to Daniel, saying, "You've been given a gift. Think about how to use it." He replied that he planned to play guitar for God.

James 5:15 The power of prayer.

¹⁵ And the prayer of faith shall save the sick, and the Lord shall raise him up;

and if he have committed sins, they shall be forgiven him.

Just before Daniel was discharged from the hospital, the doctors cautioned that he might never speak properly again due to the damage to his vocal cords. They also warned that he might not be able to eat normal and would require a special diet forever due to the sensitivity of his organs.

However, Daniel was speaking as usual within a week. As of the writing of this book, nine years have passed, and he eats anything he wants, including hot sauce. While it did take him several years to tolerate acidic foods, that sensitivity eventually disappeared.

God is good!

CHAPTER 6: EVIL SEDUCTRESS

During his time at the Christian college, Ken befriended a woman in her mid-30s while he was significantly younger. They often engaged in discussions about God and spirituality. During these conversations, she suggested that Jesus might not be the only path to heaven. Ken dismissed this notion, and their communication continued.

The woman persistently pressured Ken to "give her a baby," a request he found unsettling and was not interested in pursuing. Despite his reluctance, she continued to press him for this unusual demand until he confided in Dad and a minister at church.

The minister told Ken he was still early in his ministry journey and could be vulnerable to spiritual attacks. He expressed concern that the woman might be involved in unconventional or cult-like beliefs, urging Ken to distance himself from her.

Dad researched the woman, uncovering her obsession with Lilith and other peculiar beliefs, which aligned with the minister's suspicions. This revelation confirmed the minister's concerns.

Lilith is a figure steeped in folklore, yet she is not mentioned in the Bible. The tales surrounding her encompass themes of Adam and Eve, sexuality, and demonic associations. While this story will not delve deeper into those topics, it is essential to recognize the troubling implications of the topic.

Proverbs 5:1-6 King Solomon warns of the peril of adultery and the immoral woman.

¹ My son, attend unto my wisdom, and bow thine ear to my understanding:
² That thou mayest regard discretion, and that thy lips may keep knowledge.
³ For the lips of a strange woman drop as an honeycomb, and her mouth is smoother than oil:
⁴ But her end is bitter as wormwood, sharp as a two-edged sword.
⁵ Her feet go down to death; her steps take hold on hell.
⁶ Lest thou shouldest ponder the path of life, her ways are moveable, that thou canst not know them.

Ultimately, Ken recognized the potential threat posed by this woman and severed ties with her. The influence of demons is a genuine concern that should not be underestimated. The Bible frequently addresses the existence of demons, serving as a cautionary reminder.

1 John 4:1 Test every spirit as to whether they are from God, there are many false prophets.

¹ Beloved, believe not every spirit, but try the spirits whether they are of God: because many false prophets are gone out into the world.

CHAPTER 7: THE VENUE

Ken was well-known at a non-profit Christian music venue where the high school band often performed. As the venue underwent a management transition, they offered Ken the position of venue manager. He was thrilled about this opportunity and accepted the role.

In his new position, Ken managed to book both local and national bands and musicians, manage the sound and lighting staff, and coordinated the volunteer team. This role allowed him to meet many top Christian artists.

He started a Worship Night featuring various local worship bands. This event also included a preacher or evangelist who delivered a message.

Galatians 6:10 Seize opportunities and do good to all.

[10] As we have therefore opportunity, let us do good unto all men, especially unto them who are of the household of faith.

While overseeing the venue, Ken successfully collaborated with friends and family to orchestrate a surprise proposal for Tara, his girlfriend. With their help, the setup featured enchanting lights and music. She was invited under the pretense of helping him tidy up the venue, and to her astonishment, the proposal unfolded beautifully.

Ephesians 5:25-28 Husbands love your wives as Christ loved the church.

[25] Husbands, love your wives, even as Christ also loved the church, and gave himself for it;
[26] That he might sanctify and cleanse it with the washing of water by the word,
[27] That he might present it to himself a glorious church, not having spot, or wrinkle, or any such thing; but that it should be holy and without blemish.
[28] So ought men to love their wives as their own bodies. He that loveth his wife loveth himself.

Given his deep passion for music and worship, managing a Christian music venue was an ideal role for Ken. He led prayer with the team each night before events and led prayers for the audience, fostering a spiritual atmosphere.

Image 5 Performing at one of the Worship Nights.

CHAPTER 8: WORSHIP LEADER

During Ken's tenure managing the venue, he was presented with an exciting new opportunity: the Worship Leader position at the church's newly opening campus.

Ken, his brother Daniel, and Dad joined the launch team for this new campus, which required significant effort from everyone involved.

The campus was initially set up in an elementary school cafeteria, requiring the setup and teardown of the church every Sunday, an immense undertaking. Other churches faced similar challenges, making this experience quite common.

The school's principal told the pastor that having church in the cafeteria made a difference. She noticed children performing better in academics and staff more enlightened. This is due to God's presence in the school, and this really makes a difference.

Matthew 18:20 The church gathering at the school brought God into the establishment.

[20] For where two or three are gathered together in my name, there am I in the midst of them.

Being the worship leader was more involved than just performing on Sunday. This required planning the set, changing the arrangement, and coordinating practice with the band.

Ken and Tara found a house during this period and began buying their first home. They successfully bought a small house in what would soon become one of the most desirable neighborhoods in town. The house was financed solely in Ken's name, as they were not yet married.

The house was a fixer-upper, requiring considerable time and financial investment to prepare it for living. Ken and Tara chose not to live together primarily due to her family's strict religious beliefs.

Psalm 20:4-5 A prayer that your heart's desire would come and be granted by God.

⁴ *Grant thee according to thine own heart, and fulfil all thy counsel.*
⁵ *We will rejoice in thy salvation, and in the name of our God we will set up our banners: the Lord fulfil all thy petitions.*

Leading worship has ultimately realized Ken's long-held dream from his youth, where he once told Dad, "I really want to play worship music."

Image 6 Ken leads worship, and Daniel on guitar.

CHAPTER 9: OVERWHELMED

Ken was now leading worship and managing the music venue, having recently bought a new home they were renovating. This was a considerable burden for a young man to bear.

Those around him remained unaware of the significant stress he was experiencing. Additionally, he harbored a hidden concern that he had confided in his dad. Ken was eager to start a family, while Tara opposed having children. This disagreement only intensified his stress and anxiety.

Philippians 4:6 Do not worry about fears and anxieties.

⁶ Be careful for nothing; but in every thing by prayer and supplication with thanksgiving let your requests be made known unto God.

1 Peter 5:6-7 Cast all your anxieties on God.

⁶ Humble yourselves therefore under the mighty hand of God, that he may exalt you in due time:
⁷ Casting all your care upon him; for he careth for you.

Ken's parents were experiencing a divorce, which further intensified the stress and anxiety he was already facing.

With all that Ken was enduring, he ultimately fell victim to the insidious grip of addiction, a reality completely unknown to his friends and family.

Ken's concealed addiction was a silent bondage that subtly dominated his life, remaining hidden from view. While this may be difficult to understand, it did not diminish his devotion to God. He was engaged in a profound struggle against the evil forces within him.

Initially, Ken turned to drugs to cope with the overwhelming stress that permeated his life. A certain threshold was necessary to meet the demands placed upon him. This repeatedly led to a gradual escalation until it spiraled out of control.

The Bible holds numerous accounts of various forms of addiction, including lust, drunkenness, and greed.

Genesis 9:20-23 Noah's drunkenness.

²⁰ And Noah began to be an husbandman, and he planted a vineyard:
²¹ And he drank of the wine, and was drunken; and he was uncovered within his tent.
²² And Ham, the father of Canaan, saw the nakedness of his father, and told his two brethren without.
²³ And Shem and Japheth took a garment, and laid it upon both their shoulders, and went backward, and covered the nakedness of their father; and their faces were backward, and they saw not their father's nakedness.

2 Samuel 11:2-5 David succumbs to lust and adultery.

² And it came to pass in an eveningtide, that David arose from off his bed, and walked upon the roof of the king's house: and from the roof he saw a woman washing herself; and the woman was very beautiful to look upon.
³ And David sent and enquired after the woman. And one said, Is not this Bathsheba, the daughter of Eliam, the wife of Uriah the Hittite?
⁴ And David sent messengers, and took her; and she came in unto him, and he lay with her; for she was purified from her uncleanness: and she returned unto her house.
⁵ And the woman conceived, and sent and told David, and said, I am with child.

2 Samuel 11:14-15 Not only did David commit adultery, but he also set up her husband to die in battle.

¹⁴ *And it came to pass in the morning, that David wrote a letter to Joab, and sent it by the hand of Uriah.*
¹⁵ *And he wrote in the letter, saying, Set ye Uriah in the forefront of the hottest battle, and retire ye from him, that he may be smitten, and die.*

CHAPTER 10: REVELATION OF BONDAGE

Ken's situation had escalated to the point where he finally confided in Elliot, his best friend. Elliot tried to support him quietly through this devastating disease, but it was beyond their control.

Unfortunately, this aid came too late, as Tara discovered the problem. It was revealed that Ken was struggling with addiction.

In response, Ken sought help through counseling and a twelve-step program. Although things seemed to be improving, he experienced several setbacks.

This was challenging for Tara, leading to an argument between them. She expressed the need to take a break while he worked on regaining control over his issues.

Ken misinterpreted the seriousness of her situation and mistakenly believed she was calling off the wedding. However, that was not her intention; it was simply a misunderstanding on his part.

He decided to write a letter to his dad, explaining his addiction and his plans to look for a recovery clinic in the state. He entrusted this letter to Elliot to deliver to his dad.

He gathered everything he needed for a cross-country trip and left in the middle of the night.

Jonah 1:1-4 Jonah's disobedience as he flees the Lord and the storm ensues.

¹ Now the word of the Lord came unto Jonah the son of Amittai, saying,

²Arise, go to Nineveh, that great city, and cry against it; for their wickedness is come up before me.

³But Jonah rose up to flee unto Tarshish from the presence of the Lord, and went down to Joppa; and he found a ship going to Tarshish: so he paid the fare thereof, and went down into it, to go with them unto Tarshish from the presence of the Lord.

⁴But the Lord sent out a great wind into the sea, and there was a mighty tempest in the sea, so that the ship was like to be broken.

A hypothetical storm was approaching, much like the storm faced by Jonah.

CHAPTER 11: THE SIGN

It was morning when Elliot delivered the letter to Dad. After reading it, Dad sprang into action. Ken's mom and brothers were promptly informed of the situation and met to devise a plan.

Fortunately, everyone utilized a GPS family locator on their phones, allowing them to see that Ken had already gained a significant head start. The team sprang into action swiftly.

Dad took a moment to pray, seeking solace and guidance from Jesus for Ken's safe return and aid with his addiction. His prayer echoed the sentiments below:

"Lord Jesus,

I come to You today with a heavy heart, seeking Your comfort and guidance. I ask that You watch over Ken and keep him safe. Wherever he may be, surround him with love and protection. I beg You, Lord, to bring him home safely.

I entrust Ken's struggles with addiction to You, Lord. Nothing is impossible for You; he can be healed through Your strength and mercy.

As I leave on this journey, please keep both Daniel and me safe.

Lord Jesus, I have one more request. Please grant me a sign that Ken is safe.

In Jesus' name, I pray,
Amen."

Within a minute of finishing the prayer, Dad heard the familiar ding of his messaging app. It was a message from Ken.

"Dad, I just wanted to say I'm sorry and okay."

Overwhelmed with emotion and comforted by the Holy Spirit, Dad burst into tears. He felt certain God had answered his prayer for a "sign." This realization stirred profound feelings within him.

1 John 5:14-15 Confidence and Compassion in Prayer.

[14] *And this is the confidence that we have in him, that, if we ask any thing according to his will, he heareth us:*
[15] *And if we know that he hear us, whatsoever we ask, we know that we have the petitions that we desired of him.*

After regaining his composure, Dad gathered Daniel, and they hit the road searching for Ken.

CHAPTER 12: THE SEARCH

Dad and Daniel began tracking Ken, following the signal from his GPS. Fortunately, Ken made several stops but had already traveled halfway across the state.

The journey was stressful given the circumstances, yet Dad and Daniel persevered. While Dad drove, Daniel navigated and monitored the GPS and kept the family informed.

Several hours into their trip, the GPS signal suddenly went dark. Either Ken's phone had died, or he had disabled the locator. They managed to reach the last known location before the signal was lost.

Fortunately, Ken's primary credit card was a joint account with his dad. Reviewing the transaction history, he gleaned information about Ken's most recent whereabouts.

They were back on the road after an extended stop to determine their next move. The transaction history indicated that Ken had crossed several state lines and was now entering Louisiana.

Late in the evening, Dad received a call from an unknown number. It was the Sheriff's Department from deep within Louisiana. Apparently, Ken had been arrested, but no further details were provided.

It took several more hours to reach the location of Ken's arrest. Once there, Ken and Daniel booked a room at a local hotel in a small, unremarkable town in Louisiana.

This town was rough, as is often the case in Louisiana (apologies to Louisiana residents). They spent the night, and the following morning, they made their way to the courthouse and jail. To their dismay, they discovered that visitation was not allowed for a few days, and reservations had to be made a week in advance. Essentially, this trip had been in vain.

Dad and Daniel then returned to Dad's sister's home in Alabama, where they could unwind and rest for a few days.

Luke 15:11-17 A partial passage of The Parable of the Lost Son.

[11] And he said, A certain man had two sons:
[12] And the younger of them said to his father, Father, give me the portion of goods that falleth to me. And he divided unto them his living.
[13] And not many days after the younger son gathered all together, and took his journey into a far country, and there wasted his substance with riotous living.
[14] And when he had spent all, there arose a mighty famine in that land; and he began to be in want.
[15] And he went and joined himself to a citizen of that country; and he sent him into his fields to feed swine.
[16] And he would fain have filled his belly with the husks that the swine did eat: and no man gave unto him.
[17] And when he came to himself, he said, How many hired servants of my father's have bread enough and to spare, and I perish with hunger!

The excerpt from the Parable of the Lost Son narrates the story of a young man who leaves his home to explore distant lands.

It is strongly recommended to avoid following the example set by Ken's dad and family. The stress and heartbreak associated with such situations can be overwhelming. Entrusting this matter to God and engaging in frequent prayer is essential.

CHAPTER 13: THE TROOPER

After Ken's confinement, the circumstances surrounding his arrest were revealed. The reported details indicate that Ken had stopped to tweak his drug and was extremely intoxicated. He was pulled over on the side of the interstate but remained in the travel lane.

A highway patrol trooper stopped to assess the situation, but Ken drove off, initiating a slow-speed chase that lasted for several miles and crossed county lines. At this point, multiple police and highway patrol vehicles joined the pursuit.

The police had set up stop strips to disable Ken's vehicle. However, he drove through them, puncturing all four tires, yet he continued to attempt his escape.

As the car became increasingly difficult to control, Ken pulled over to the side of the highway. The police quickly surrounded the vehicle with their guns drawn.

An officer knocked on Ken's window, prompting him to pull forward. A trooper positioned in front of the vehicle had to leap out of the way sustaining minor injuries to avoid being struck. Ken remained oblivious to the danger he posed.

Multiple officers and troopers later stated that they felt justified in firing their weapons, considering the vehicle as a deadly weapon. Surprisingly, no shots were fired.

Despite the justification, the decision not to fire upon Ken may have been an act of "providence," leaving little room for alternative explanations.

Isaiah 54:17 No weapon formed against you shall prosper.

[17] *No weapon that is formed against thee shall prosper; and every tongue that shall rise against thee in judgment thou shalt condemn. This is the heritage of the servants of the Lord, and their righteousness is of me, saith the Lord.*

The police and troopers successfully rammed into his vehicle, effectively barricading it to bring it to a halt. Ken eventually stopped, and the officers extracted him from his vehicle without any resistance. Several police vehicles sustained damage during the operation.

The news media had already arrived at the scene to document the thrilling events unfolding in this remote town. This incident quickly made headlines, as it was the most captivating occurrence in quite some time.

Ken was taken into custody and booked at the county's local jail, where the arrest occurred. This facility was known to be one of the most severe in Louisiana.

CHAPTER 14: THE LOST

O nce Ken was escorted into the crowded jail cell, he endured the customary initiation beating from the other inmates, which was a shocking experience for him as a non-violent person.

As Ken began to adjust to his incarceration, his body gradually started to detoxify. Sleep proved elusive due to the rowdy and noisy behavior of the inmates. Daily fights erupted among them, prompting the guards to throw in canisters of tear gas, often laughing at the ensuing chaos.

As previously mentioned, the facility was exceptionally harsh, lacking windows or air conditioning. The oppressive Louisiana heat and humidity exacerbated the already unpleasant conditions.

At least once a week, a local preacher would visit the facility. He would stand at the door outside the cell, passionately shouting fire and brimstone passages. Despite his fervent delivery, the inmates would disregard his message as though he were invisible. Nevertheless, the preacher continued to yell at the top of his lungs, undeterred by their indifference.

Eventually, Ken emerged from his shell and interacted with a few inmates. He shared his love for God, revealing that he was a worship leader and musician. He also mentioned his previous role as a manager of a music venue before this current ordeal.

Ken formed friendships with several inmates and engaged them in discussions about God, which led to him organizing what could be described as small group meetings. He began to minister to these lost souls, who were incarcerated for a range of offenses, from serious crimes to minor infractions.

Matthew 25:34-40 A parable urging Christians to help those in need no matter the situation.

[34] *Then shall the King say unto them on his right hand, Come, ye blessed of my Father, inherit the kingdom prepared for you from the foundation of the world:*
[35] *For I was an hungred, and ye gave me meat: I was thirsty, and ye gave me drink: I was a stranger, and ye took me in:*
[36] *Naked, and ye clothed me: I was sick, and ye visited me: I was in prison, and ye came unto me.*
[37] *Then shall the righteous answer him, saying, Lord, when saw we thee an hungred, and fed thee? or thirsty, and gave thee drink?*
[38] *When saw we thee a stranger, and took thee in? or naked, and clothed thee?*
[39] *Or when saw we thee sick, or in prison, and came unto thee?*
[40] *And the King shall answer and say unto them, Verily I say unto you, Inasmuch as ye have done it unto one of the least of these my brethren, ye have done it unto me.*

Ken sensed the presence of the Holy Spirit in the cell as many inmates engaged in the small group meetings. However, a few inmates chose to remain isolated and refrained from participating.

After Ken successfully engaged many of the inmates in his ministry, the local preacher made another appearance. As he began his impassioned sermon, a noticeable change occurred this time. Most inmates knelt at the door, attentively listening to his message. With tears streaming down his face, the preacher raised his arms to the heavens, fervently praising the Lord. He believed he had guided these lost souls to salvation.

Isaiah 61:1 The good news of salvation to the prisoners.

[1] *The Spirit of the Lord God is upon me; because the Lord hath anointed me to preach good tidings unto the meek; he hath sent me to bind up the brokenhearted, to proclaim liberty to the captives, and the opening of the prison to them that are bound;*

CHAPTER 15: FREEDOM

Ken's parents frequently visited Louisiana to visit him and attend court dates. In this rural Cajun town, if you couldn't afford a lawyer, the public defenders would often delay court appearances for inmates for an extended period.

The lawyers available for hire were the same individuals serving as public defenders. If you paid them, they would fulfill their responsibilities; otherwise, they would remain inactive.

They managed to secure a competent lawyer on retainer, and he began working on the case. Their strategy involved requesting a jury trial and consistently seeking continuances at each court appearance. The goal was to prolong the proceedings, allowing media attention to wane over time.

2 Peter 2:19 The promise of freedom.

[19] While they promise them liberty, they themselves are the servants of corruption: for of whom a man is overcome, of the same is he brought in bondage.

The passage is appropriate for this context. Although Ken's lawyer offered him outstanding support, his performance as a public defender was comparable to that of his colleagues; regrettably, it proved to be ineffective.

Afterward, Ken was released on bail and granted temporary freedom. His parents were filled with joyful tears as Ken exited the courthouse.

Luke 15:20-24 The ending passage of The Parable of the Lost Son.

20 And he arose, and came to his father. But when he was yet a great way off, his father saw him, and had compassion, and ran, and fell on his neck, and kissed him.
21 And the son said unto him, Father, I have sinned against heaven, and in thy sight, and am no more worthy to be called thy son.
22 But the father said to his servants, Bring forth the best robe, and put it on him; and put a ring on his hand, and shoes on his feet:
23 And bring hither the fatted calf, and kill it; and let us eat, and be merry:
24 For this my son was dead, and is alive again; he was lost, and is found. And they began to be merry.

During one of the court appearances, the inmate Snake from the first chapter made his entrance, still shackled. Ken and his parents sat in the audience as Snake was led into the courtroom through a back entrance. The moment Snake locked eyes with Ken, a sinister recognition passed between them, causing Ken to shudder in fear at the sight of this evil figure. The judge sentenced him to life in prison, a fate Snake had anticipated.

Another inmate, who had been incarcerated alongside Ken, also made an appearance. This unfortunate individual had been convicted of stealing a moon pie from a local convenience store and received an 8-month sentence. However, he had already served nearly a year while awaiting trial. Ultimately, he was granted time served and released.

After the session concluded, several lawyers, including Ken's attorney, were heard laughing at the situation's absurdity; mocking the man for receiving an 8-month sentence for a moon pie theft, despite having already served a year.

Luke 16:13 The parable of the unjust servant.

13 No servant can serve two masters: for either he will hate the one, and love the other; or else he will hold to the one, and despise the other. Ye cannot serve God and mammon.

The town where Ken was released on bond was a Christian community. Despite the unscrupulous nature of the lawyers involved, the community upheld strong moral values. Due to Ken's connection with the church and his evident devotion to God, he was offered a plea deal that involved some restitution and reduced charges.

Additionally, there was a final step to resolve his charges in another county he encountered during his ordeal. This county also agreed to lower the charges and successfully negotiated a more reasonable restitution.

Freedom had finally become a reality.

CHAPTER 16: HYPOCRITES

O nce Ken arrived home, the weight of his situation struck him profoundly. His relationship with his fiancée, Tara, was permanently over. At the time, he failed to recognize that this was a blessing in disguise.

While he was incarcerated, Tara had urged Ken to sign over the house, which was financed in his name, convincing him it was the right course of action. However, during a visit from his parents, they persuaded him to reconsider. Although Ken found this decision difficult, he ultimately agreed with their advice. Tara was infuriated by his choice, as this house had been her dream home.

Proverbs 21:9 The value of peace and harmony within the family.

⁹ It is better to dwell in a corner of the housetop, than with a brawling woman in a wide house.

Ken also lost his job at the Christian music venue due to his unbearable and embarrassing actions. The owner of the venue, a respectable Christian man, chose to remain friends with Ken afterward.

In addition to losing his job, he also lost his position as worship leader, which was a significant blow for him, and he struggled to cope.

Members of the church were deeply disappointed by Ken's situation and reacted worse than anyone he knew. The gossip surrounding his circumstances was rampant, and their behavior was highly unprofessional. It's essential to understand that the individuals or members do not represent the church as a whole; therefore, when there are bad apples and bigots within a congregation, it is unfair to blame the church or the denomination.

Leviticus 19:15-18 Do not slander against your neighbor.

[15] 'Ye shall do no unrighteousness in judgment: thou shalt not respect the person of the poor, nor honor the person of the mighty: but in righteousness shalt thou judge thy neighbour.
[16] Thou shalt not go up and down as a talebearer among thy people: neither shalt thou stand against the blood of thy neighbour; I am the Lord.
[17] Thou shalt not hate thy brother in thine heart: thou shalt in any wise rebuke thy neighbour, and not suffer sin upon him.
[18] Thou shalt not avenge, nor bear any grudge against the children of thy people, but thou shalt love thy neighbour as thyself: I am the Lord.

Ken's true friends handled the situation admirably, standing by him throughout this challenging time. In contrast, other friends and acquaintances were less forgiving, revealing themselves to be anything but true friends.

Rather than creating a new social media profile, Ken maintained his existing one, valuing his connections from the music scene, church affiliations, and genuine friendships. Unfortunately, he had to unfriend several hundred individuals because of the incident, many of whom were members of his church.

To keep his home, Ken permitted his brother Chase to move in and rent from him while he lived with their dad.

In summary, he faced significant losses: his fiancée, his job, his position as a worship leader, numerous so-called friends, and nearly his home.

CHAPTER 17: RECOVERY

Following Ken's release, he became involved with a Christian Recovery Center, participating as an outpatient rather than a resident, which was affiliated with his church.

During his time there, Ken's spirituality and commitment to God deepened significantly. He developed meaningful friendships with both the staff and fellow patients.

He began playing worship sets at the recovery center alongside a friend and associate from the church. Together, they would perform music, and someone would deliver a message.

This center utilized a twelve-step program like those of Alcoholics Anonymous, Narcotics Anonymous, or Celebrate Recovery. Ken diligently engaged with the steps, and in turn, the steps proved effective for him.

Isaiah 38:16-17 God restores to health after sickness.

[16] O Lord, by these things men live, and in all these things is the life of my spirit: so wilt thou recover me, and make me to live.
[17] Behold, for peace I had great bitterness: but thou hast in love to my soul delivered it from the pit of corruption: for thou hast cast all my sins behind thy back.

Ken actively participated in feeding the homeless at the recovery center, and during the holidays, his whole family would join him in volunteering. This experience was deeply rewarding for all those involved.

Luke 14:13-14 I invite the poor, crippled, lame, and blind to his feasts.

¹³ *But when thou makest a feast, call the poor, the maimed, the lame, the blind:*
¹⁴ *And thou shalt be blessed; for they cannot recompense thee: for thou shalt be recompensed at the resurrection of the just.*

Ken had never publicly declared his faith through baptism until he was baptized at the church, marking a moment of immense pride.

While this discussion will not delve into the details of the twelve steps, as they are widely accessible, we will focus on the first and twelfth steps.

The first step emphasizes the importance of admitting powerlessness over addiction and recognizing that one's life has become unmanageable. This acknowledgment is crucial for any alcoholic or addict, as it is the first step toward seeking help and achieving recovery.

The twelfth step highlights the importance of spiritual awakening and encourages individuals to share these steps with other alcoholics and addicts. It is crucial to support and minister to those struggling with addiction.

During this time, Ken began dating Hannah, a long-time acquaintance. Both were employed at a local restaurant and before long, Hannah became pregnant. They were thrilled about the prospect of bringing a child into the world.

CHAPTER 18: THE BABY

The moment Hannah and Ken knew they were expecting a baby was a profound turning point in their lives. A blend of excitement, joy, and a sprinkle of anxiety set the stage for a journey unlike any other. As the news sinks in, a whirlwind of emotions takes over, and the reality of bringing a new life into the world begins to unfold.

Psalm 127:3 Children are a gift from the Lord.

[3] Lo, children are an heritage of the Lord: and the fruit of the womb is his reward.

During the first ultrasound, they caught a glimpse of the baby's tiny heartbeat, a moment etched in memory forever. It was the first connection to the life growing inside her.

The first gentle kick was a reminder that your little one is growing stronger each day. Around this time another ultrasound revealed the baby was a girl.

Planning for the baby became a delightful task. From choosing a name to decorating the nursery, every decision felt significant. Creating baby registries at their favorite stores. The anticipation built as they imagined the day they could finally hold your baby in their arms.

The day finally arrives when labor begins. It mixes anticipation and adrenaline as they head to the hospital. The childbirth experience is unique for everyone, filled with pain, joy, and overwhelming love. As they hold your baby for the first time, the world around them fades away, and all that matters is the tiny life they have brought into the world.

John 16:21 The pain of labor would soon turn to joy.

[21] *A woman when she is in travail hath sorrow, because her hour is come: but as soon as she is delivered of the child, she remembereth no more the anguish, for joy that a man is born into the world.*

The name they decided on was *Adelaide*, the title of one of Ken's favorite songs from a popular Christian band. Little Adelaide was the most beautiful baby they had ever seen.

As they settled into life with baby Adelaide, the transition to parenthood was both exhilarating and daunting. Each day brought new challenges and milestones, from the first smile to the first steps. It was a journey of learning, patience, and unconditional love. Support from family and friends becomes invaluable as they share in the joys and help navigate the complexities of caring for a newborn.

In this chapter of your life, you will discover strengths you never knew you had. The bond you form with your child will shape your identity and redefine your priorities. Parenthood was a growth journey, not just for the baby but for them as well.

As they reflect on the experience of having a baby, they realize that it is not just about the arrival of a new life but about their own transformation. It is a journey filled with love, laughter, and lessons that will last a lifetime.

Image 7 Adelaide holds the most significant place in his life.

CHAPTER 19: WORSHIP AGAIN

Ken began working for a Worship Consulting Service, which provides musicians, ministers, and other professionals to churches seeking temporary staffing solutions.

Returning to the stage to worship the Lord gave Ken a sense of fulfillment and redemption from his challenges.

Ephesians 1:7 Redemption through His blood.

[7] In whom we have redemption through his blood, the forgiveness of sins, according to the riches of his grace;

This position enabled Ken to play both drums and guitar while leading worship at numerous churches. The same company also employed his brother Daniel, but they seldom performed at the same church.

Ken played at several churches for extended periods. A few of these offered him permanent positions; however, they typically involved long commutes.

Playing at various churches and denominations provided Ken with significant exposure to the differences in doctrine and theology. He performed at many different denominations of churches, including Baptist, Methodist, Non-Denominational, and Anglican churches.

Ken began leading worship at a local church, a small

congregation with a surfer preacher, located in a movie theater. Like his previous experiences, this role required him to set up and tear down every Sunday.

This church offered him a permanent position as the worship leader, with Daniel on guitar. He accepted the role, but the Consulting Service had contractual issues. Fortunately, the church managed to reach an agreement without needing to buy out his contract.

Ken played at this church for a considerable time but chose to leave when a position at another church, conveniently located close to home, became available.

The new church featured an exceptional preacher and a talented worship team. Ken led worship there while his dad managed the projection. This church quickly felt like home, and its proximity was a significant advantage.

Acts 20:28 The Holy Spirit has made you overseers of the church of God.

²⁸ Take heed therefore unto yourselves, and to all the flock, over the which the Holy Ghost hath made you overseers, to feed the church of God, which he hath purchased with his own blood.

Ken began playing drums for a highly regarded country band, recognized as the region's finest and most professional act. After joining the band, he had the opportunity to minister to its members, including a non-believer known as Caveman, who has since developed a relationship with God. The band now prays before each performance, with Ken taking the lead in prayer.

Hebrews 6:10 God will not forget the work of you ministering to others.

¹⁰ For God is not unrighteous to forget your work and labour of love, which ye have shewed toward his name, in that ye have ministered to the saints, and do minister.

Image 8 Leading worship at his new permanent church.

Image 9 The country band now prays before each set.

CHAPTER 20: THE ACCIDENT

It's several years later and during late baseball season, Ken and his younger brother Chase were watching a game together, while Ken also texted the pastor about it.

They decided to take a drive down the street, bringing along Ken's dog, Mindy, for a little adventure.

About a mile from home, the road curved slightly. Unfortunately, they were going a bit too fast, causing the car to lose control, spin, and crash into a tree on the driver's side.

Chase and Mindy were ejected from the vehicle, but Ken was not as fortunate; he became trapped beneath the car, resulting in an immediate and painless death.

Meanwhile, their older brother Daniel noticed emergency vehicles passing their house and realized, through Ken's GPS, that they hadn't moved in quite some time. He attempted to drive down the road to investigate, but the police had already closed it off.

Daniel then called their dad to report what he had seen. Dad and his fiancée quickly jumped in the car and drove across town. By the time they arrived, the ambulance had just left. An officer informed Dad that one person had been taken to the hospital while another had tragically passed away.

Dad's heart sank at the news. No parent wants to endure the loss of a child; the pain was unbearable, the worst experience anyone could imagine.

Matthew 5:4 Those who mourn will be comforted.

⁴ Blessed are they that mourn: for they shall be comforted.

Dad hurried to the hospital and entered the ER to find Chase lying on a bed. It was then that he understood Ken had passed away.

Approaching Chase, his dad delivered the heartbreaking news. Overwhelmed, Chase clutched the cross around Dad's neck, tearing it off in his distress. From that moment on, Dad could never wear the cross again, as it was forever tied to painful memories.

Ken was laid to rest at the church cemetery. The ceremony was beautiful with many people in attendance.

Psalm 34:18 God helps us bear the burden of grief.

¹⁸ The Lord is nigh unto them that are of a broken heart; and saveth such as be of a contrite spirit.

Image 10 Ken's final worship set was truly awe-inspiring.

CHAPTER 21: THE FIRE

Five months had passed since Ken's passing, but the grief lingered. One day, Dad received a phone call about an accident at Chase's house and was asked to check it out. Since he was nearby, he went there immediately.

When he arrived in the neighborhood, he saw the road was barricaded, and Chase's house was engulfed in flames. Walking down the street, a neighbor informed him that Chase had been taken to the trauma center.

Chase's father notified the family about the situation and went to pick up his fiancée from work. Together, they hurried to the trauma center.

At the center, they waited anxiously for news from the doctors. After an eternity, the doctors arrived to update them on Chase's condition.

Chase had sustained severe burns over most of his body and needed to be rushed to a burn center in a nearby city.

Knowing it would be some time before Chase arrived, everyone returned home to prepare for a long hospital stay and the hour-long drive to the burn center.

Upon arriving at the burn center, the family was informed that Chase had burns covering 90% of his body, and he was in critical condition.

Certain members of the family were able to scrub down and enter his room. It was a sight no one would wish upon their father. He was entirely bandaged except for his face and toes. Chase's face was severely burned and swollen to twice its normal size.

The doctors informed the family that he had been placed in a medically induced coma while they continued to treat his burns. This treatment persisted for several days, but progress was minimal. Some family members would stay late before returning home to get some rest.

After seven days, the doctors delivered devastating news. Chase had been on life support, and his vital signs had deteriorated significantly. He had shown no brain activity for the past several hours, and the doctors wanted the family to consider the difficult decision of unplugging him.

Although the family may have anticipated this outcome, the news was incredibly difficult to accept. The loss of two sons in just five months is an unbearable tragedy.

The decision to remove Chase from life support was a difficult one, but ultimately, it was made to end his suffering.

Romans 8:38-39 Nothing can separate us from God's love

[38] For I am persuaded, that neither death, nor life, nor angels, nor principalities, nor powers, nor things present, nor things to come,
[39] Nor height, nor depth, nor any other creature, shall be able to separate us from the love of God, which is in Christ Jesus our Lord.

The nurses entered the room, inviting the family to say their final goodbyes. However, Dad declined to enter, stating that he had already said farewell and did not wish to witness Chase's passing.

The following morning, Dad visited Chase's house to survey the damage. The scene was harrowing, with the house showing significant destruction.

As he exited the bedroom where the fire had started and moved into the living area, he noticed handprints on the wall, evidence of Chase's desperate attempt to find his way to the door.

Once outside, a neighbor approached and shared additional details. When Chase emerged, he collapsed in the front yard, and another neighbor covered him with a blanket while waiting for emergency responders to arrive. Once emergency responders arrived, Chase began shouting for his dog. He desperately wanted someone to go in and rescue his pet, but that was impossible. The responders provided medical assistance and quickly transported him to the trauma center.

Psalm 147:3 God understands your grief and will offer comfort

³ He healeth the broken in heart, and bindeth up their wounds.

Image 11 Chase loved the outdoors.

CHAPTER 22: THE AFTERMATH

Most worship team members wore black without coordination on the Sunday preceding the incident. The pastor humorously remarked, "Is this Johnny Cash Day?"

Several other worship team members expressed that the worship set was flawless the Sunday before the incident.

Dad drove by the site the day after the accident, and the radio fell silent. There were orange flowers and candles placed around the site with two orange butterflies hovering over the site.

One night following the accident, Alexa started playing a song. Daniel asked his father if he was there playing the music, which Dad replied he was across town. He looked up Alexa history and found the song *Light at the End of the Tunnel*.

While the Bible primarily focuses on the Holy Spirit, it does not provide explanations for other spirits. However, it frequently mentions spirits, reflecting the beliefs of people in biblical times who acknowledged various spiritual entities. In translations, these spirits are referred to as "phantasma".

Matthew 14:26 The disciples see Jesus walking on the sea and think He's a ghost.

²⁶ *And when the disciples saw him walking on the sea, they were troubled, saying, It is a spirit; and they cried out for fear.*

36 And as they thus spake, Jesus himself stood in the midst of them, and saith unto them, Peace be unto you.
37 But they were terrified and affrighted, and supposed that they had seen a spirit.
38 And he said unto them, Why are ye troubled? and why do thoughts arise in your hearts?
39 Behold my hands and my feet, that it is I myself: handle me, and see; for a spirit hath not flesh and bones, as ye see me have.

To this day, years after his passing, the country band Ken drummed in still prays before every set.

Adelaide's future is secured thanks to Ken's legacy. The country band received sponsorship from a prestigious boat company, contributing funds to an escrow account dedicated to Adelaide's education. As Ken's sole heir, Adelaide benefits from her mother Hannah's decision to sell Ken's house, resulting in a significant profit that is also allocated to another escrow account for her benefit.

The crash site remained barren, devoid of grass or weeds for over three years. Ken's dad believes this absence was a divine message, indicating that a true servant was taken from us too soon.

James 4:14 Nobody knows what will happen tomorrow.

14 Whereas ye know not what shall be on the morrow. For what is your life? It is even a vapour, that appeareth for a little time, and then vanisheth away.

Kenneth Bradford significantly impacted the world, guiding many towards salvation. His legacy and devotion to God will continue to resonate long after his departure.

AFTERWORD

This book is written in the third person, reflecting my perspective as a father. The process of writing this story was profoundly challenging due to the emotions it evoked. I found myself crying more during the creation of this book than I have in many years.

I want to emphasize that prayer alone cannot alleviate your grief. Grief is an essential part of the healing journey, and crying is equally important in this process, even for men.

As I conclude the text of this book, it has been over four years since I lost my boys. Instead of crying daily, my tears now come only when I reflect on the loss or the traumatic events that transpired.

I speak about my boys daily, focusing on the joyful moments and cherished memories. It is crucial to steer clear of the painful aspects, particularly their deaths. While that brings sadness, the happy memories uplift me, making it feel as though they are still with me.

Consider the unimaginable experience of losing two children within five months. Without God, many would resort to antidepressants or worse. Some individuals who have lost a child may turn to alcohol and addiction for the rest of their lives.

On January 1st, as I finalized this book, I also faced the loss of my dog, Condi. She was a birthday gift 11 years ago and brought so much joy with her playful spirit.

What God has granted me is the strength to navigate this

without succumbing to alcohol or other vices.

May God bless Teresa (my wife), my three boys, Condi, and my entire family.

Image 12 The crash site.

Image 13 Together again.

ABOUT THE AUTHOR

 Larry Briscoe is a dedicated servant with over 10 years of service in ministry, driven by a deep faith and a heart for others. Throughout his journey, Larry has navigated profound personal loss, including the heartbreaking deaths of two sons, which has shaped his understanding of grief, resilience, and divine comfort. His experiences have led him to witness numerous accounts of God's providence and what he believes to be miraculous interventions, deepening his conviction in the power of faith and prayer. Larry's ministry is fueled by a passion for sharing these transformative experiences and the hope they offer to others facing adversity. His story is one of profound loss, unwavering faith, and the miraculous ways God shows up amid suffering.

INDEX

i

ii

www.ingramcontent.com/pod-product-compliance
Lightning Source LLC
Chambersburg PA
CBHW050903120626
46554CB00003B/981